The Smart Air Fryer Cookbook

Quick, Tasty and Affordable Low-Fat Recipes to Cook at Home with Your Air Fryer

Linda Wang

© **Copyright 2021 by Linda Wang - All rights reserved.**

The content contained within this book may not be reproduced, duplicated or transmitted without direct written permission from the author or the publisher.
Under no circumstances will any blame or legal responsibility be held against the publisher, or author, for any damages, reparation, or monetary loss due to the information contained within this book. Either directly or indirectly.

Legal Notice:
This book is copyright protected. This book is only for personal use. You cannot amend, distribute, sell, use, quote or paraphrase any part, or the content within this book, without the consent of the author or publisher.

Disclaimer Notice:
Please note the information contained within this document is for educational and entertainment purposes only. All effort has been executed to present accurate, up to date, and reliable, complete information. No warranties of any kind are declared or implied. Readers acknowledge that the author is not engaging in the rendering of legal, financial, medical or professional advice. The content within this book has been derived from various sources. Please consult a licensed professional before attempting any techniques outlined in this book.
By reading this document, the reader agrees that under no circumstances is the author responsible for any losses, direct or indirect, which are incurred as a result of the use of information contained within this document, including, but not limited to, — errors, omissions, or inaccuracies.

TABLE OF CONTENTS

INTRODUCTION 1

Spinach Egg Breakfast 5

Air Fryer Breakfast Frittata 7

Bacon Grilled Cheese 9

Sausage Breakfast Casserole 11

Brioche Sausage 13

Tuna Sandwiches 15

Garlic Kale 17

Chicken and Asparagus 19

Tomato and Avocado 20

Okra and Green Beans Stew 22

Mozzarella and Tomato Bruschetta 23

Cashew and Chicken Manchurian 25

Green Beans 27

Parmesan Zucchini Chips 29

Rosemary Potato Chips 31

Yummy Cheesy Rice Balls 33

Lime Trout and Shallots 35

Oregano Clams 37

Mussels and Shrimp 39

Buttermilk Brined Turkey Breast 41

Spicy Green Crusted Chicken	43
Almond Chicken	45
Special Salsa Chicken Steak	47
Stuffed Chicken and Baked Potatoes	49
Delicious Meatloaf	51
Pickle Fried Chicken	53
Honey Chicken Wings	55
Rosemary Pork and Artichokes	57
Pork Tenderloin with Bell Peppers	59
Pork Rolls	61
Baked Egg and Veggies	63
Broccoli And Tomato Sauce	65
Ratatouille	67
Coconut Chicken Soup	69
Herbed Carrots (Vegan)	71
Spices Stuffed Eggplants (Vegan)	73
Cheese Bread	75
Peppers and Cheese Dip	76
Buffalo Chicken Dip	77
Lemon Cookies	79
Sweet Zucchini Bread	81
Lemon Mousse	83
Lemon Cake	85

Cranberry Jam 86

Chocolate Pudding 88

Butter Cookies 90

Apple Pie in Air Fryer 92

Blueberry & Lemon Cake 94

Fudge Brownies 97

Blackberry Crisp 99

NOTES 101

INTRODUCTION

An Air Fryer is a magic revolutionized kitchen appliance that helps you fry with less or even no oil at all. This kind of product applies Rapid Air technology, which offers a new way to fry with less oil. This new invention cooks food through the circulation of superheated air and generates 80% low-fat food. Although the food is fried with less oil, you don't need to worry as the food processed by the Air Fryer still has the same taste like the food fried using the deep-frying method.

This technology uses a superheated element, which radiates heat close to the food and an exhaust fan in its lid to circulate airflow. An Air Fryer ensures that the food processed is cooked completely. The exhaust fan located at the top of the cooking chamber helps the food get the same heating temperature in every part quickly, resulting in a cooked food of better and healthier quality. Besides, cooking with an Air Fryer is also suitable for those individuals which are too busy or do not have enough time. For example, an Air Fryer only needs half a spoonful of oil and takes 10 minutes to serve a medium bowl of crispy French fries.

In addition to serving healthier food, an Air Fryer also provides some other benefits to you. Since an Air Fryer helps you fry using less oil or without oil for some kind of food, it automatically reduces the fat and cholesterol content in food. Indeed, no one will refuse to enjoy fried food without worrying about the greasy and fat content. Having fried food with no guilt is one of the pleasures of life. Besides having low fat and cholesterol, you save some amount of money by consuming oil sparingly, which can be used for other needs. An Air Fryer also can reheat your food. Sometimes, when you have fried leftover and you reheat it, it will usually serve reheated greasy food with some addition of unhealthy reuse oil. Undoubtedly, the saturated fat in the fried food gets worse because of this process. An Air Fryer helps you reheat your food without being afraid of extra oils that the food may absorb. Fried bananas, fish and chips, nuggets, or even fried chicken can be reheated to become as warm and crispy as they were before by using an Air Fryer.

Some people may think that spending some amount of money to buy a fryer is wasteful. I dare to say that they are wrong because an Air Fryer is not only used to fry. It is a sophisticated multi-function appliance since it also helps you to roast chicken, make steak, grill fish, and even bake a cake. With a built-in air filter, an Air Fryer filters the air and saves your kitchen from smoke and grease.

An air Fryer is really a new innovative method of cooking. Grab it fast and welcome to a clean and healthy kitchen.

Spinach Egg Breakfast

Preparation Time: 10 minutes

Cooking Time: 20 minutes

Serve: 4

Ingredients:

- 3 eggs
- 1/4 cup coconut milk

- 4 oz spinach, chopped
- 1/4 cup parmesan cheese, grated
- 3 oz cottage cheese

Directions:

1. Preheat the air fryer to 350 °F.
2. Add eggs, milk, half parmesan cheese, and cottage cheese in a bowl and whisk well. Add spinach and stir well.
3. Pour mixture into the air fryer baking dish.
4. Sprinkle remaining half parmesan cheese on top.
5. Place dish in the air fryer and cook for 20 minutes.
6. Serve and enjoy.

Nutrition:

Calories 144, Fat 8.5 g, Carbohydrates 2.5 g, Sugar 1.1 g, Protein 14 g, Cholesterol 135 mg

Air Fryer Breakfast Frittata

Preparation Time: 15 minutes

Cooking Time: 20 minutes

Servings: 2

Ingredients:

- 4 eggs, lightly beaten
- ¼ pound breakfast sausage, fully cooked and crumbled

- ½ cup Monterey Jack cheese, shredded
- 2 tablespoons red bell pepper, diced
- 1 green onion, chopped
- 1 pinch cayenne pepper

Directions:

1. Preheat the Air fryer to 365 °F and grease a nonstick 6x2-inch cake pan.
2. Whisk together eggs with sausage, green onion, bell pepper, cheese and cayenne in a bowl.
3. Transfer the egg mixture in the prepared cake pan and place in the Air fryer.
4. Cook for about 20 minutes and serve warm.

Nutrition:

Calories: 464, Fat: 33.7g, Carbohydrates: 10.4g, Sugar: 7g, Protein: 30.4g, Sodium: 704mg

Bacon Grilled Cheese

Preparation Time: 5 minutes

Cooking Time: 7 minutes

Servings: 2

Ingredients:

- 4 slices of bread
- 2 slices mozzarella cheese
- 1 tablespoon butter, softened
- 2 slices mild cheddar cheese
- 6 slices bacon, cooked
- 1 tablespoon olive oil

Directions:

1. Preheat the Air fryer to 370 degrees F and grease an Air fryer basket with olive oil.
2. Spread butter onto one side of each bread slice and place in the Air Fryer basket.
3. Layer with cheddar cheese slice, followed by bacon, mozzarella cheese and close with the other bread slice.

4. Place in the Air fryer and cook for about 4 minutes.
5. Flip the sandwich and cook for 3 more minutes.
6. Remove from the Air fryer and serve.

Nutrition:

Calories: 518, Fat: 34.9g, Carbohydrates: 20g, Sugar: 0.6g, Protein: 29.9g, Sodium: 1475mg

Sausage Breakfast Casserole

Preparation Time: 10 minutes

Cooking Time: 20 minutes

Servings: 4

Ingredients:

- 1 pound ground breakfast sausage
- 3 bell peppers, diced
- 1 pound hash browns
- ¼ cup sweet onion, diced
- 4 eggs
- 1 tablespoon olive oil
- Salt and black pepper, to taste

Directions:

1. Preheat the Air fryer to 355 degrees F and grease the casserole dish with olive oil.
2. Place the hash browns on the bottom of the casserole dish and top with sausages, bell peppers and onions.

3. Transfer into the Air fryer and cook for about 10 minutes.
4. Crack eggs into the casserole dish and cook for 10 more minutes.
5. Season with salt and black pepper and serve warm.

Nutrition:

Calories: 472, Fat: 25g, Carbohydrates: 47.6g, Sugar: 6.8g, Protein: 15.6g, Sodium: 649mg

Brioche Sausage

Preparation time: 10 minutes,

Cooking time: 15 minutes;

Serve: 4

Ingredients:

- 2 sausages
- 2 bread sticks

Direction:

1. Remove the crumb from the bread to obtain a hollow cylinder (make pieces of about 10 cm, otherwise it will be difficult to work them).
2. Place the sausage in half the bread, then make slices about 2 cm thick.
3. Place the slices at the bottom of the basket (6 per batch).
4. Set the temperature to 160 °C.
5. Cook for 10 minutes, turning the crispy rolls on themselves after 5/6 minutes.
6. Serve while it is still hot.

Nutrition:

Calories 546, Carbohydrates 37g , Fat 35g, Sugars 6g, Protein 20g, Cholesterol 0mg

Tuna Sandwiches

Preparation Time: 14 minutes

Servings: 4

Ingredients:

- 6 bread slices
- 16 oz. canned tuna; drained
- 6 provolone cheese slices
- 2 spring onions; chopped.
- 1/4 cup mayonnaise
- 1 tbsp. lime juice
- 2 tbsp. mustard
- 3 tbsp. butter; melted

Directions:

1. In a bowl, mix the tuna, mayo, lime juice, mustard and spring onions; stir until combined.
2. Spread the bread slices with the butter, place them in the preheated air fryer and bake them at 350 °F for 5 minutes
3. Spread tuna mix on half of the bread slices and top with the cheese and the other bread slices
4. Place the sandwiches in your air fryer's basket and cook for 4 minutes more. Divide between plates and serve.

Garlic Kale

Preparation Time: 10 minutes

Cooking time: 20 minutes

Servings: 4

Ingredients:

- 1 pound kale leaves, torn
- 1 teaspoon coriander, ground
- 1 tablespoon avocado oil

- 1 teaspoon basil, dried
- 1 tablespoon balsamic vinegar
- 4 garlic cloves, minced
- Salt and black pepper to the taste

Directions:

1. In your air fryer, combine the kale with the oil and the other ingredients, toss well and cook them at 370 degrees F for 20 minutes.
2. Divide the mix between plates and serve as a side dish.

Nutrition:

Calories 66, fat 5, fiber 8, carbs 11, protein 6

Chicken and Asparagus

Preparation Time: 25 minutes

Servings: 4

Ingredients:

- 1 bunch asparagus; trimmed and halved
- 4 chicken breasts, skinless; boneless and halved
- 1 tbsp. olive oil
- 1 tbsp. sweet paprika
- Salt and black pepper to taste.

Directions:

1. Take a bowl and mix all the ingredients, toss, put them in your Air Fryer's basket and cook at 390 °F for 20 minutes
2. Divide between plates and serve.

Nutrition:

Calories: 230; Fat: 11g; Fiber: 3g; Carbs: 5g; Protein: 12g

Tomato and Avocado

Preparation Time: 8 minutes

Servings: 4

Ingredients:

- ½ lb. cherry tomatoes; halved
- 2 avocados, pitted; peeled and cubed
- 1/3 cup coconut cream
- 1 ¼ cup lettuce; torn
- A pinch of salt and black pepper
- Cooking spray

Directions:

1. Grease the air fryer with cooking spray, combine the tomatoes with avocados, salt, pepper and the cream and cook at 350 °F for 5 minutes shaking once
2. In a salad bowl, mix the lettuce with the tomatoes and avocado mix, toss and serve.

Nutrition:

Calories: 226; Fat: 12g; Fiber: 2g; Carbs: 4g; Protein: 8g

Okra and Green Beans Stew

Preparation Time: 20 minutes

Servings: 4

Ingredients:

- 1 cup okra
- 1 lb. green beans; halved
- 4 garlic cloves; minced
- 3 tbsp. tomato sauce
- 1 tbsp. thyme; chopped.
- Salt and black pepper to taste.

Directions:

1. In a pan that fits your air fryer, mix all the ingredients, toss, introduce the pan in the air fryer and cook at 370 °F for 15 minutes
2. Divide the stew into bowls and serve.

Nutrition:

Calories: 183; Fat: 5g; Fiber: 2g; Carbs: 4g; Protein: 8g

Mozzarella and Tomato Bruschetta

Preparation Time: 10 minutes

Servings: 3

Ingredients:

- 3 ounces grated mozzarella cheese
- 6 small french loaf slices
- 1/2 cup finely chopped tomatoes

- 1 tablespoon. fresh basil; chopped
- 1 tablespoon olive oil

Directions:

1. Preheat the Air Fryer to 350 - degrees Fahrenheit. Cook the bread for about 3 minutes.
2. Top with tomato, mozzarella, and prosciutto.
3. Drizzle the olive oil over this.
4. Place the bruschetta in the Air Fryer and cook for an additional minute. Serve and enjoy.

Cashew and Chicken Manchurian

Preparation Time: 30 minutes

Servings: 3

Ingredients:
- 1 cup chicken boneless
- One Egg
- 6 cashew nuts
- 1 teaspoon ginger [chopped]
- 1 spring onions [chopped]
- 1 onion [chopped]
- 3 green chili
- 1/2 teaspoon garlic [chopped]
- 2 tablespoon flour
- 1 tablespoon cornstarch
- 1 teaspoon soy sauce
- 2 teaspoon chili paste
- 1 teaspoon pepper
- 1 pinch msg & sugar
- water as needed

- 1 tablespoon oil

Directions:

1. Coat chicken with egg, salt and pepper. Mix cornstarch and flour, coat chicken and cook at preheated to 360 - degrees Fahrenheit Air Fryer for 10 minutes.
2. Cook nuts with oil in a pan.
3. Add onions and cook until translucent. Add the remaining ingredients and cook sauce.
4. Add chicken and garnish with spring onions.

Green Beans

Preparation Time: 25 minutes

Servings: 4

Ingredients:

- 6 cups green beans; trimmed
- 1 tbsp. hot paprika
- 2 tbsp. olive oil
- A pinch of salt and black pepper

Directions:

1. Take a bowl and mix the green beans with the other ingredients, toss, put them in the air fryer's basket and cook at 370 °F for 20 minutes
2. Divide between plates and serve as a side dish.

Nutrition:

Calories: 120; Fat: 5g; Fiber: 1g; Carbs: 4g; Protein: 2g

Parmesan Zucchini Chips

Preparation Time: 20 minutes

Servings: 4

Ingredients:

- 1 oz. pork rinds.
- 2 medium zucchini
- ½ cup grated Parmesan cheese.
- 1 large egg.

Directions:

1. Slice zucchini in ¼-inch-thick slices. Place between two layers of paper towels or a clean kitchen towel for 30 minutes to remove excess moisture
2. Place pork rinds into food processor and pulse until finely ground. Pour into medium bowl and mix with Parmesan
3. Beat egg in a small bowl.
4. Dip zucchini slices in egg and then in pork rind mixture, coating as completely as possible.

Carefully place each slice into the air fryer basket in a single layer, working in batches as necessary.

5. Adjust temperature to 320 Degrees F and set the timer for 10 minutes. Flip chips halfway through the cooking time. Serve warm.

Nutrition:

Calories: 121; Protein: 9.9g; Fiber: 0.6g; Fat: 6.7g; Carbs: 3.8g

Rosemary Potato Chips

Preparation Time: 1 hour 15 minutes

Servings: 2

Ingredients:

- 4 medium russet potatoes
- 1 tablespoon olive oil
- 2 teaspoon rosemary; chopped
- 2 pinches salt

Directions:

1. Scrub the potatoes under running water to clean.
2. Cut the potatoes lengthwise and peel them into thin chips directly into a mixing bowl full of water.
3. Soak the potatoes for 30 minutes; changing the water several times. Drain thoroughly and pat completely dry with a paper towel.

4. Preheat the Air Fryer to 330 - degrees Fahrenheit. In a mixing bowl; toss the potatoes with olive oil. Place them into the cooking basket and cook for 30 minutes or until golden brown, shaking frequently to ensure the chips are cooked evenly.
5. When finished and still warm, toss in a large bowl with rosemary and salt.

Yummy Cheesy Rice Balls

Preparation Time: 40 minutes

Servings: 3

Ingredients:

- 1 cup rice [boiled]
- 1 cup paneer
- 1 tablespoon corn flour
- 1 green chili; chopped
- 1 cup cheese mozzarella; cubed
- 2 tablespoon carrot; chopped
- 2 tablespoon sweet corn
- 1 tablespoon corn flour slurry
- salt to taste
- garlic powder [optional] to taste
- 1/2 breadcrumbs
- 1 teaspoon oregano

Directions:

1. Preheat Air Fryer to 390 - degrees Fahrenheit.
2. Mix all the above-mentioned ingredients and form into small ball shape.
3. Roll the mixture in slurry and breadcrumbs. Cook for 15 minutes.

Lime Trout and Shallots

Preparation Time: 17 minutes

Servings: 4

Ingredients:

- 4 trout fillets; boneless
- 3 garlic cloves; minced

- 6 shallots; chopped.
- ½ cup butter; melted
- Juice of 1 lime
- ½ cup olive oil
- A pinch of salt and black pepper

Directions:

1. In a pan that fits the air fryer, combine the fish with the shallots and the rest of the ingredients, toss gently
2. Put the pan in the machine and cook at 390 °F for 12 minutes, flipping the fish halfway.
3. Divide between plates and serve with a side salad.

Nutrition:

Calories: 270; Fat: 12g; Fiber: 4g; Carbs: 6g; Protein: 12g

Oregano Clams

Preparation time: 20 minutes

Servings: 4

Ingredients:

- Shucked clams: 2 dozen
- Dried oregano: 1 tsp.
- Chopped parsley: .25 cup
- Grated parmesan cheese: .25 cup
- Unseasoned breadcrumbs: 1 cup
- Melted butter: 4 tbsp.
- Minced garlic cloves: 3
- For the Pan: Sea salt: 1 cup

Directions:

1. Warm up the Air Fryer a few minutes at 400º Fahrenheit.
2. Mince the garlic and combine with the breadcrumbs, oregano, parsley, parmesan cheese, and melted butter in a medium mixing bowl.

3. Using a heaping tablespoon of the crumb mixture, add it to the clams.
4. Fill the insert with salt, arrange the clams inside, and air fry for three minutes.
5. Garnish with fresh parsley and lemon wedges.

Mussels and Shrimp

Preparation Time: 25 minutes

Servings: 4

Ingredients:
- 20 oz. canned tomatoes; chopped.
- 1½ lbs. large shrimp; peeled and deveined
- 1/2 cup parsley; chopped.
- 1/2 tsp. marjoram; dried

- 1 tbsp. basil; dried
- 12 mussels
- 8 oz. clam juice
- 2 tbsp. butter; melted
- 2 yellow onions; chopped.
- 3 garlic cloves; minced
- Salt and black pepper to taste

Directions:

1. Place all the ingredients in a pan that fits your air fryer; toss well
2. Put the pan into the fryer and cook at 380 °F for 15 minutes. Divide into bowls and serve right away.

Buttermilk Brined Turkey Breast

Preparation Time: 15 minutes

Cooking Time: 20 minutes

Servings: 8

Ingredients:

- 3½ pounds boneless, skinless turkey breast
- ¾ cup brine from a can of olives
- 2 fresh thyme sprigs
- 1 fresh rosemary sprig
- ½ cup buttermilk

Directions:

1. Preheat the Air fryer to 350 degrees F and grease an Air fryer basket.
2. Mix olive brine and buttermilk in a bowl until well combined.
3. Place the turkey breast, buttermilk mixture and herb sprigs in a resealable plastic bag.
4. Seal the bag and refrigerate for about 12 hours.

5. Remove the turkey breast from bag and arrange the turkey breast into the Air fryer basket.
6. Cook for about 20 minutes, flipping once in between.
7. Dish out the turkey breast onto a cutting board and cut into desired size slices to serve.

Nutrition:

Calories: 215, Fat: 3.5g, Carbohydrates: 9.4g, Sugar: 7.7g, Protein: 34.4g, Sodium: 2000mg

Spicy Green Crusted Chicken

Preparation Time: 10 minutes

Cooking Time: 40 minutes

Servings: 6

Ingredients:

- 1 pound chicken pieces
- 6 eggs, beaten
- 6 teaspoons parsley
- 4 teaspoons thyme
- 6 teaspoons oregano
- 4 teaspoons paprika
- Salt and freshly ground black pepper, to taste

Directions:

1. Preheat the Air fryer to 360 degrees F and grease an Air fryer basket.
2. Whisk eggs in a bowl and mix all the ingredients in another bowl except chicken pieces.

3. Dip the chicken in eggs and then coat generously with the dry mixture.
4. Arrange half of the chicken pieces in the Air fryer basket and cook for about 20 minutes.
5. Repeat with the remaining mixture and dish out to serve hot.

Nutrition:

Calories: 218, Fat: 10.4g, Carbohydrates: 2.6g, Sugar: 0.6g, Protein: 27.9g, Sodium: 128mg

Almond Chicken

Preparation time: 10 - 20,

Cooking time: 15 – 30;

Serve: 6

Ingredients:

- 500 g chicken breast
- ½ onion
- 130g crushed almonds

- 1 tbsp grated fresh ginger
- 60 g of soy sauce
- Water (sufficient quantity)

Direction:

1. Pour the almonds into the basket.
2. Roast the almonds for 5 minutes at 150 ºC.
3. Remove the almonds and pour the chopped onion and ginger, the oil into the tank and brown for about 2 minutes.
4. Add lightly floured chicken, salt, pepper and cook for additional 13 minutes.
5. Pour the soy sauce, a ladle of hot water, the roasted almonds and simmer for additional 5 minutes.

Nutrition:

Calories 458, Fat 34g, Carbohydrates 22g, Sugars 7.3g, Protein 20g, Cholesterol 24mg

Special Salsa Chicken Steak

Preparation Time: 10 minutes

Cooking Time: 30 minutes

Servings: 6

Ingredients:

- 2 pounds chicken steak
- 1 cup tomato sauce
- ½ cup shredded Monterey Jack cheese
- 2 cups salsa
- ½ teaspoon garlic powder
- ½ teaspoon hot pepper sauce
- Salt and black pepper, to taste

Directions:

1. Preheat the Air fryer to 450 degrees F and grease an Air fryer basket.
2. Season the chicken steak with garlic powder, salt and black pepper and marinate for about 8 hours.

3. Mix salsa, tomato sauce and hot pepper sauce in a bowl.
4. Arrange the steak pieces in the Air fryer basket and drizzle with the salsa mixture.
5. Cook for about 30 minutes and dish out to serve hot.

Nutrition:

Calories: 345, Fat: 14.3g, Carbohydrates: 7.6g, Sugar: 4.3g, Protein: 45.1g, Sodium: 828mg

Stuffed Chicken and Baked Potatoes

Preparation time: 10-20,

Cooking time: 45-60;

Serve: 4

Ingredients:

- 800 g boneless chicken
- 150 g sausage
- 300 g minced meat
- 80 g French toast
- 1 tbsp chopped parsley

Direction:

1. Bone the chicken (or bone directly by the butcher).
2. Prepare the filling:
3. Put in a food processor the meat, the sausage, the French toast bathed in milk to soften it, the parsley, the eggs, the grated cheese, the salt, the pepper and mix until obtaining a homogeneous and compact mixture.

4. Fill the boneless chicken and tie it well with a kitchen rope so that the filling does not come out.
5. Place the chicken inside the bowl, add the chopped potatoes, oil, salt, and pepper.
6. Set the air fryer to 160 °C. Cook everything for 60 minutes over mix the potatoes 2-3 times to cook evenly and turn the chicken about once in the middle of cooking.

Nutrition:

Calories 223.8, Fat 6.5 g, Carbohydrate 19.8 g, Sugars 1.9 g, Protein21.2 g, Cholesterol 48.8 mg

Delicious Meatloaf

Preparation Time: 10 minutes

Cooking Time: 32 minutes

Serve: 8

Ingredients:

- 2 eggs
- 1/2 cup parmesan cheese, grated
- 1/2 cup marinara sauce, without sugar

- 1 lb mozzarella cheese, cut into cubes
- 1 cup cottage cheese
- 2 lbs ground turkey
- 2 tsp Italian seasoning
- 1/4 cup basil pesto
- 1 tsp salt

Directions:

1. Preheat the air fryer to 370 F.
2. Add all ingredients into the large bowl and mix until well combined.
3. Transfer bowl mixture to the silicone loaf pan and place in the air fryer.
4. Cook for 32 minutes.
5. Serve and enjoy.

Nutrition:

Calories 350, Fat 19.5 g, Carbohydrates 4 g, Sugar 2 g, Protein 43 g, Cholesterol 175 mg

Pickle Fried Chicken

Cooking Time: 47 minutes

Servings: 4

Ingredients:

- 4 chicken legs; bone in, skin on, cut into drumsticks and thighs, about 3 ½ lbs.
- 2 eggs
- 1/2 cup almond flour
- Pickle juice from 24 oz. jar of kosher dill pickles
- 1 cup breadcrumbs
- 1 tsp. black pepper
- 1 tsp. sea salt
- 2 tbsp. olive oil
- 1/8 tsp. cayenne pepper
- 1/2 tsp. ground paprika

Directions:

1. Place chicken in a bowl and pour the pickle juice over it. Cover and transfer chicken to fridge to brine in pickle juice for 8 hours

2. Remove the chicken from the fridge. Place flour in a bowl and season it with salt and pepper. In another bowl, whisk egg and olive oil.
3. Place the breadcrumbs in a third bowl, along with paprika, salt, pepper and cayenne pepper. Preheat your air fryer to 370 °F. Remove the chicken from the pickle brine and pat dry
4. Coat pieces of chicken with flour, then egg mixture and finally with breadcrumbs. Place the breaded chicken on a baking sheet and spray each piece with cooking spray. Air fry chicken in two batches.
5. Place two pieces thighs and two drumsticks into air fryer basket. Air fry for 10 minutes. Turn pieces of chicken over and cook for another 10 minutes
6. Remove chicken and set aside. Repeat with the second batch of chicken. Lower the temperature to 340 °F.
7. Place the first batch of chicken on top of the second batch and air fry for an additional 7 minutes.

Honey Chicken Wings

Cooking Time: 30 minutes

Servings: 2

Ingredients:

- 1 lb. chicken wings; tips removed and wings separated.
- Cilantro; chives, or scallions for garnish

For the sauce

- 1/4 cup honey
- 1 ½ tbsp. soy sauce
- 1 tbsp. butter
- 2 tbsp. sriracha sauce
- Juice of ½ a lime

Directions:

1. Preheat the air fryer to 360 °F. Add the chicken wings to the air fryer basket and cook for 30 minutes, turning the chicken about every 7 minutes with tongs to make sure the wings are

evenly browned

2. While the wings are cooking, add the sauce ingredients to a small sauce pan and bring to a boil for about 3 minutes. When the wings are cooked, toss them in a bowl with the sauce until fully coated. Sprinkle with the garnish and serve immediately.

Rosemary Pork and Artichokes

Preparation time: 10 minutes

Cooking time: 25 minutes

Servings: 4

Ingredients:

- 1pound pork stew meat, cubed
- 1cup canned artichoke hearts, drained and halved

- 2 tablespoons rosemary, chopped
- 2 tablespoons olive oil
- ½ teaspoon cumin, ground
- ½ teaspoon nutmeg, ground
- ½ cup sour cream
- Salt and black pepper to the taste

Directions:

1. In a pan that fits your air fryer, mix the pork with the artichokes and the other ingredients, introduce in the fryer and cook at 400 degrees F for 25 minutes.
2. Divide everything into bowls and serve.

Nutrition:

Calories 280, Fat 13, Fiber 9, Carbs 22, Protein 18

Pork Tenderloin with Bell Peppers

Servings: 3

Preparation Time: 20 minutes

Cooking Time: 15 minutes

Ingredients

- 1 large red bell pepper, seeded and cut into thin strips
- 1 red onion, thinly sliced
- 2 teaspoons Herbs de Provence
- 1 tablespoon olive oil
- 10½-ounces pork tenderloin, cut into 4 pieces
- ½ tablespoon Dijon mustard
- Salt and ground black pepper, as required

Directions:

1. In a bowl, add the bell pepper, onion, Herbs de Provence, salt, black pepper, and ½ tablespoon of oil and toss to coat well.
2. Rub the pork pieces with mustard, salt, and black pepper.

3. Drizzle with the remaining oil.
4. Set the temperature of air fryer to 390 degrees F. Grease an air fryer pan.
5. Place bell pepper mixture into the prepared Air Fryer pan and top with the pork pieces.
6. Air fry for about 15 minutes, flipping once halfway through.
7. Remove from air fryer and transfer the pork mixture onto serving plates.
8. Serve hot.

Nutrition:

Calories: 218, Carbohydrate: 7.1g, Protein: 27.7g, Fat: 8.8g, Sugar: 3.7g, Sodium: 110mg

Pork Rolls

Servings: 4

Preparation Time: 20 minutes

Cooking Time: 15 minutes

Ingredients

- 1 scallion, chopped
- ¼ cup sun-dried tomatoes, finely chopped
- 2 tablespoons fresh parsley, chopped
- Salt and ground black pepper, as required
- 4: 6-ounces pork cutlets, pounded slightly
- 2 teaspoons paprika
- ½ tablespoon olive oil

Directions:

1. In a bowl, mix well scallion, tomatoes, parsley, salt, and black pepper.
2. Spread the tomato mixture over each pork cutlet.
3. Roll each cutlet and secure with cocktail sticks.

4. Rub the outer part of rolls with paprika, salt and black pepper.
5. Coat the rolls evenly with oil.
6. Set the temperature of air fryer to 390 degrees F. Grease an air fryer basket.
7. Arrange pork rolls into the prepared air fryer basket in a single layer.
8. Air fry for about 15 minutes.
9. Remove from air fryer and transfer the pork rolls onto serving plates.
10. Serve hot.

Nutrition:

Calories: 244, Carbohydrate: 14.5g, Protein: 20.1g, Fat: 8.2g, Sugar: 1.7g, Sodium: 708mg

Baked Egg and Veggies

Preparation Time: 20 minutes

Servings: 2

Ingredients:

- 1 cup fresh spinach; chopped
- 2 large eggs.
- 1 small zucchini, sliced lengthwise and quartered
- 1 medium Roma tomato; diced
- ½ medium green bell pepper; seeded and diced
- 2 tbsp. salted butter
- ¼ tsp. garlic powder.
- ¼ tsp. onion powder.
- ½ tsp. dried basil
- ¼ tsp. dried oregano.

Directions:

1. Grease two: 4-inchramekins with 1 tbsp. butter each.

2. Take a large bowl, toss zucchini, bell pepper, spinach and tomatoes. Divide the mixture in two and place half in each ramekin.
3. Crack an egg on top of each ramekin and sprinkle with onion powder, garlic powder, basil and oregano. Place into the air fryer basket. Adjust the temperature to 330 Degrees F and set the timer for 10 minutes. Serve immediately.

Nutrition:

Calories: 150; Protein: 8.3g; Fiber: 2.2g; Fat: 10.0g; Carbs: 6.6g

Broccoli And Tomato Sauce

Preparation Time: 20 minutes

Servings: 4

Ingredients:
- 1 broccoli head, florets separated
- ¼ cup scallions; chopped
- ½ cup tomato sauce
- 1 tbsp. sweet paprika

- 1 tbsp. olive oil
- Salt and black pepper to taste.

Directions:

1. In a pan that fits the air fryer, combine the broccoli with the rest of the Ingredients, toss.
2. Put the pan in the fryer and cook at 380 °F for 15 minutes
3. Divide between plates and serve.

Nutrition:

Calories: 163; Fat: 5g; Fiber: 2g; Carbs: 4g; Protein: 8g

Ratatouille

Preparation Time: 30 minutes

Servings: 4

Ingredients:

- 1 yellow bell pepper, seeded and chopped
- 1 zucchini; chopped
- 1 eggplant; chopped
- 3 tomatoes; chopped
- 2 garlic cloves, minced
- 2 small onions; chopped
- 1 green bell pepper, seeded and chopped
- 1 tbsp. balsamic vinegar
- 2 tbsp. Herbs de Provence
- 1 tbsp. olive oil
- Salt and ground black pepper; as your liking

Directions:

1. Set the temperature of air fryer to 355 °F. Grease a baking dish.

2. In a large bowl; add the vegetables, garlic, Herbs de Provence, oil, vinegar, salt and black pepper and toss to coat well.
3. Transfer vegetable mixture into the prepared baking dish. Arrange the baking dish into air fryer and air fry for about 15 minutes.
4. Remove from air fryer and transfer the vegetable mixture into a serving bowl. Serve immediately.

Coconut Chicken Soup

Preparation Time: 5 minutes

Cooking Time: 15 minutes

Servings: 4

Ingredients:

- 1 lb. chicken thighs, boneless and cut into chunks
- 2 cups Swiss chard, chopped
- 1 tsp. turmeric
- 1 ½ cups celery stalks, chopped
- 1 tbsp. chicken broth base
- 10 oz. can tomato
- 1 cup coconut milk
- 1 tbsp. ginger, grated
- 4 garlic cloves, minced
- 1 onion, chopped

Directions:

1. Add ½ cup of coconut milk, broth base, turmeric, tomatoes, ginger, garlic and onion to the blender; blend until smooth.
2. Transfer blended the mixture to the air fryer along with Swiss chard, celery and chicken. Stir well.
3. Secure pot with lid and cook on manual high pressure for 5 minutes.
4. Allow pressure to release naturally for 10 minutes, then release using quick release Directions.
5. Add remaining coconut oil and stir well.
6. Serve and enjoy.

Nutrition:

Calories – 473 Protein – 39.5 g. Fat – 23.9 g. Carbs – 29.7 g.

Herbed Carrots (Vegan)

Servings: 8

Preparation Time: 15 minutes

Cooking Time: 14 minutes

Ingredients

- 6 large carrots, peeled and sliced lengthwise
- ½ tablespoon fresh oregano, chopped
- 2 tablespoons olive oil
- ½ tablespoon fresh parsley, chopped
- Salt and ground black pepper, as required

Directions:

1. Set the temperature of air fryer to 360 degrees F. Grease an air fryer basket.
2. In a bowl, mix together the carrot slices, and oil.
3. Arrange carrot slices into the prepared air fryer basket in a single layer.
4. Air fry for about 12 minutes.

5. Remove from air fryer and sprinkle the carrots evenly with herbs, salt and black pepper.
6. Air fry for 2 more minutes.
7. Remove from air fryer and transfer the carrot slices onto serving plates.
8. Serve hot.

Nutrition:

Calories: 53, Carbohydrate: 5.5g, Protein: 0.5g, Fat: 3.5g, Sugar: 2.7g, Sodium: 57mg

Spices Stuffed Eggplants (Vegan)

Preparation Time: 15 minutes

Cooking Time: 12 minutes

Servings: 4

Ingredients:

- 8 baby eggplants
- 4 teaspoons olive oil, divided
- ¾ tablespoon ground coriander

- ¾ tablespoon dry mango powder
- ½ teaspoon ground cumin
- ½ teaspoon ground turmeric
- ½ teaspoon garlic powder
- Salt, to taste

Directions:

1. Preheat the Air fryer to 370 degrees F and grease an Air fryer basket.
2. Make 2 slits from the bottom of each eggplant leaving the stems intact.
3. Mix one teaspoon of oil and spices in a bowl and fill each slit of eggplants with this mixture.
4. Brush the outer side of each eggplant with the remaining oil and arrange in the Air fryer basket.
5. Cook for about 12 minutes and dish out in a serving plate to serve hot.

Nutrition:

Calories: 317, Fats: 6.7g, Carbohydrates: 65g, Sugar: 33g, Proteins: 10.9g, Sodium: 61mg

Cheese Bread.

Preparation Time: 20 minutes

Servings: 2

Ingredients:

- 1 large egg.
- ¼ cup grated Parmesan cheese.
- 1 cup shredded mozzarella cheese
- ½ tsp. garlic powder.

Directions:

1. Mix all ingredients in a large bowl. Cut a piece of parchment to fit your air fryer basket. Press the mixture into a circle on the parchment and place into the air fryer basket
2. Adjust the temperature to 350 Degrees F and set the timer for 10 minutes.

Nutrition:

Calories: 258; Protein: 19.2g; Fiber: 0.1g; Fat: 16.6g; Carbs: 3.7g

Peppers and Cheese Dip

Preparation Time: 25 minutes

Servings: 6

Ingredients:

- 2 bacon slices, cooked and crumbled
- 4 oz. parmesan; grated
- 8 oz. cream cheese, soft
- 4 oz. mozzarella; grated
- 2 roasted red peppers; chopped.
- A pinch of salt and black pepper

Directions:

1. In a pan that fits your air fryer, mix all the ingredients and whisk really well.
2. Introduce the pan in the fryer and cook at 400°F for 20 minutes. Divide into bowls and serve cold

Nutrition:

Calories: 173; Fat: 8g; Fiber: 2g; Carbs: 4g; Protein: 11g

Buffalo Chicken Dip

Preparation Time: 20 minutes

Servings: 4

Ingredients:

- 1 ½ cups shredded medium Cheddar cheese, divided.
- 2 scallions, sliced on the bias
- 8 oz. full-fat cream cheese; softened.
- 1 cup cooked; diced chicken breast
- ½ cup buffalo sauce
- ⅓ cup chopped pickled jalapeños.
- ⅓ cup full-fat ranch dressing

Directions:

1. Place chicken into a large bowl. Add cream cheese, buffalo sauce and ranch dressing. Stir until the sauces are well mixed and mostly smooth. Fold in jalapeños and 1 cup Cheddar.

2. Pour the mixture into a 4-cup round baking dish and place remaining Cheddar on top. Place dish into the air fryer basket.
3. Adjust the temperature to 350 Degrees F and set the timer for 10 minutes. When done, the top will be brown and the dip bubbling. Top with sliced scallions. Serve warm.

Nutrition:

Calories: 472; Protein: 25.6g; Fiber: 0.6g; Fat: 32.0g; Carbs: 9.1g

Lemon Cookies

Preparation Time: 30 minutes

Servings: 12

Ingredients:

- ¼ cup cashew butter, soft
- 1 egg, whisked
- ¾ cup swerve
- 1 cup coconut cream
- 1 tsp. baking powder
- Juice of 1 lemon
- 1 tsp. lemon peel, grated

Directions:

1. In a bowl, combine all the ingredients gradually and stir well.
2. Spoon balls this on a cookie sheet lined with parchment paper and flatten them.
3. Put the cookie sheet in the fryer and cook at 350°F for 20 minutes. Serve the cookies cold

Nutrition:

Calories: 121; Fat: 5g; Fiber: 1g; Carbs: 4g; Protein: 2g

Sweet Zucchini Bread

Preparation Time: 10 minutes

Cooking time: 40 minutes

Servings: 12

Ingredients:

- 3 eggs, whisked
- 1 cup zucchini, shredded
- 2 cups almond flour
- 2 teaspoons baking powder
- ½ cup coconut oil, melted
- ¾ cup swerve
- 1 teaspoon lemon juice
- 1 teaspoon vanilla extract
- 1 tablespoon lemon zest
- Cooking spray

Directions:

1. In a bowl, mix all the Ingredients: except the cooking spray and stir well.

2. Grease a loaf pan that fits the air fryer with the cooking spray, line with parchment paper and pour the loaf mix inside.
3. Put the pan in the air fryer and cook at 330 degrees F for 40 minutes.
4. Cool down, slice and serve.

Nutrition:

Calories 143, fat 11, fiber 1, carbs 3, protein 3

Lemon Mousse

Preparation Time: 15 minutes

Cooking Time: 10 minutes

Servings: 6

Ingredients:

- 12-ounces cream cheese, softened
- 1 teaspoon lemon liquid stevia

- 1/3 cup fresh lemon juice
- 1½ cups heavy cream
- ¼ teaspoon salt

Directions:

1. Preheat the Air fryer to 345 degrees F and grease a large ramekin lightly.
2. Mix all the ingredients in a large bowl until well combined.
3. Pour into the ramekin and transfer into the Air fryer.
4. Cook for about 10 minutes and pour into the serving glasses.
5. Refrigerate to cool for about 3 hours and serve chilled.

Nutrition:

Calories: 305, Fat: 31g, Carbohydrates: 2.6g, Sugar: 0.4g, Protein: 5g, Sodium: 279mg

Lemon Cake

Preparation Time: 22 minutes

Servings: 6

Ingredients:

- 3 eggs
- 3 oz. brown sugar
- 3 oz. flour
- 1 tsp. dark chocolate; grated
- 3½ oz. butter; melted
- 1/2 tsp. lemon juice

Directions:

1. Mix all of the ingredients in a bowl.
2. Pour the mixture into a greased cake pan and place in the fryer
3. Cook at 360 °F for 17 minutes. Let cake cool before serving

Cranberry Jam

Preparation Time: 25 minutes

Servings: 8

Ingredients:

- 2 lbs. cranberries
- 4 oz. black currant
- 3 tbsp. water
- 2 lbs. sugar

- Zest of 1 lime

Directions:

1. In a pan that fits your air fryer, add all the ingredients and stir.
2. Place the pan in the fryer and cook at 360 °F for 20 minutes. Stir the jam well, divide into cups, refrigerate and serve cold

Chocolate Pudding

Preparation Time: 34 minutes

Servings: 4

Ingredients:

- 2 medium eggs
- 1/4 cup fresh orange juice
- 2/3 cup dark chocolate; chopped

- 1/2 cup butter
- 1/4 cup caster sugar
- 2 tbsp. self-rising flour
- 2 tsp. fresh orange rind, finely grated

Directions:

1. In a microwave-safe bowl; add the butter and chocolate. Microwave on high heat for about 2 minutes or until melted completely, stirring after every 30 seconds. Remove from microwave and stir the mixture until smooth. Add the sugar and eggs and whisk until frothy
2. Add the orange rind and juice, followed by flour and mix until well combined. Set the temperature of air fryer to 355 °F. Grease 4 ramekins.
3. Divide mixture into the prepared ramekins about ¾ full. Air fry for about 12 minutes
4. Remove from the air fryer and set aside to completely cool before serving. Serve warm

Butter Cookies

Preparation Time: 10 minutes

Cooking time: 20 minutes

Servings: 12

Ingredients:

- 2 eggs, whisked
- 1 tablespoon heavy cream

- ½ cup butter, melted
- 2 teaspoons vanilla extract
- 2 and ¾ cup almond flour
- Cooking spray
- ¼ cup swerve

Directions:

1. In a bowl, mix all the Ingredients: except the cooking spray and stir well.
2. Shape 12 balls out of this mix, put them on a baking sheet that fits the air fryer greased with cooking spray and flatten them.
3. Put the baking sheet in the air fryer and cook at 350 degrees F for 20 minutes.
4. Serve the cookies cold.

Nutrition:

Calories 234, fat 13, fiber 2, carbs 4, protein 7

Apple Pie in Air Fryer

Servings: 4

Cooking Time: 35 minutes

Ingredients

- 1 beaten egg
- ½ teaspoon vanilla extract
- 1 large apple, chopped
- 1 Pillsbury Refrigerator pie crust
- 1 tablespoon butter
- 1 tablespoon ground cinnamon
- 1 tablespoon raw sugar
- 2 teaspoons lemon juice
- 2 tablespoon sugar
- Baking spray

Directions:

1. Lightly grease baking pan of air fryer with cooking spray. Spread pie crust on bottom of pan up to the sides.

2. In a bowl, mix vanilla, sugar, cinnamon, lemon juice, and apples. Pour on top of pie crust. Top apples with butter slices.
3. Cover apples with the other pie crust. Pierce with knife the tops of pie.
4. Spread beaten egg on top of crust and sprinkle sugar.
5. Cover with foil.
6. For 25 minutes, cook on 390 °F.
7. Remove foil cook for 10 minutes at 330 °F until tops are browned.
8. Serve and enjoy.

Nutrition:

Calories: 372; Carbs: 44.7g; Protein: 4.2g; Fat: 19.6g

Blueberry & Lemon Cake

Servings: 4

Cooking Time: 17 minutes

Ingredients

- 2 eggs
- 1 cup blueberries
- zest from 1 lemon
- juice from 1 lemon
- 1 tsp. vanilla
- brown sugar for topping: a little sprinkling on top of each muffin-less than a teaspoon
- 1/2 cup cream
- 2 1/2 cups self-rising flour
- 1/2 cup Monk Fruit: or use your preferred sugar
- 1/4 cup avocado oil: any light cooking oil

Directions:

1. In mixing bowl, beat well wet Ingredients. Stir in dry ingredients and mix thoroughly.
2. Lightly grease baking pan of air fryer with cooking spray. Pour in batter.

3. For 12 minutes, cook on 330 ºF.
4. Let it stand in air fryer for 5 minutes.
5. Serve and enjoy.

Nutrition:

Calories: 589; Carbs: 76.7g; Protein: 13.5g; Fat: 25.3g

Fudge Brownies

Servings: 8

Preparation Time: 15 minutes

Cooking Time: 20 minutes

Ingredients

- 2 eggs
- ½ cup butter, melted
- ½ cup flour
- 1 cup sugar
- 1/3 cup cocoa powder
- 1 teaspoon baking powder
- 1 teaspoon vanilla extract

Directions:

1. Set the temperature of Air fryer to 350 degrees F. Grease a baking pan.
2. In a large bowl, add the sugar, and butter and whisk until light and fluffy.
3. Add the remaining ingredients and mix until well combined.

4. Place mixture evenly into the prepared pan and with the back of spatula, smooth the top surface.
5. Arrange the baking pan into an air fryer basket.
6. Air fry pan for about 20 minutes.
7. Remove the baking pan from air fryer and set aside to cool completely.
8. Cut into 8 equal-sized squares and serve.

Nutrition:

Calories: 250, Carbohydrate: 33.4g, Protein: 13g, Fat: 13.2g, Sugar: 25.2g, Sodium: 99mg

Blackberry Crisp

Preparation Time: 20 minutes

Servings: 4

Ingredients:

- 2 cups blackberries
- 1 cup Crunchy Granola
- ⅓ cup powdered erythritol

- 2 tbsp. lemon juice
- ¼ tsp. xanthan gum

Directions:

1. Take a large bowl, toss blackberries, erythritol, lemon juice and xanthan gum.
2. Pour into 6-inch round baking dish and cover with foil. Place into the air fryer basket.
3. Adjust the temperature to 350 Degrees F and set the timer for 12 minutes.
4. When the timer beeps, remove the foil and stir.
5. Sprinkle granola over mixture and return to the air fryer basket. Adjust the temperature to 320 Degrees F and set the timer for 3 minutes or until top is golden. Serve warm.

Nutrition:

Calories: 496; Protein: 9.2g; Fiber: 12.5g; Fat: 42.1g; Carbs: 44.0g

Notes

www.ingramcontent.com/pod-product-compliance
Lightning Source LLC
Chambersburg PA
CBHW070932080526
44589CB00013B/1488